Swamp Isthmus

Other works by Joshua Marie Wilkinson:

Suspension of a Secret in Abandoned Rooms
Lug Your Careless Body out of the Careful Dusk: a poem in fragments
The Book of Whispering in the Projection Booth
Selenography
The Courier's Archive & Hymnal

Swamp Isthmus

by Joshua Marie Wilkinson

Black Ocean
Boston · New York · Chicago

Black Ocean
P.O. Box 52030
Boston, MA 02205
blackocean.org

ISBN 978-1-939568-00-7

Wilkinson, Joshua Marie.
  Swamp isthmus / Joshua Marie Wilkinson.
     pages cm
  ISBN 978-1-939568-00-7
  I. Title.
  PS3623.I5526S93 2013
  811'.6-dc23
                                   2013000489

FIRST EDITION

ACKNOWLEDGEMENTS

Excerpts of this work have appeared in *580 Split, Black Warrior Review, Cannibal, Colorado Review, Columbia Poetry Review, Front Porch, Glitter Pony, Gulf Coast, Handsome, Jubilat, Little Red Leaves, Luna, No Tell Motel, Octopus, Packingtown Review, Sonora Review, West Wind Review, Whiskey Island, & Zoland Poetry Annual.*

"Cold Faction" and an excerpt of "I go by Edgar Huntly" were published as eponymous chapbooks by Further Adventures Press (Chicago 2009) & DoubleCross Press (Minneapolis 2009), respectively. A warm thank you to all the editors, and especially to B.J. Love and MC Hyland. I thank my friends who offered their support: Solan Jensen, David Rubin, Abraham Smith, Brent Hendricks, Kate Bernheimer, SRM, Patrick Culliton, LLB, Mathias Svalina, Jane Miller, NEG, & Pond. "A Saint Among the Stragglers' Beds" is for Noah Saterstrom, whose drawing in *Figures for a Darkroom Voice* inspired it. My infinite gratitude to Janaka Stucky (who made this book better), and to Carrie Olivia Adams, Nikkita Cohoon, & A. Minetta Gould—everybody at Black Ocean: thank you.

Swamp Isthmus is Book 2 in the *No Volta* pentalogy.

for Zachary Schomburg & Brandon Shimoda

TABLE OF CONTENTS

The resigned factions of the dead preside.

—Hart Crane

Cordial Disappearances

we stand in
for the moon

carry
a slide rule
to the yard under

logging noise
takes practice how
to carefully open

this door
with your eyes down
& your colors intact

we put our clothes
back on

slowly before

our laughter turns us
into somebody else's

lumbering up
limberlost
to map in
lines of so-called
becoming

polaroids of
crumbs

without messengers

lining us up
against us

the moon gets horrible
in the yard

the yard repents
& a delivery

gets made anyhow

no curtains to shut us down

this weather
is our own

even if it
rubs the names
to clover

more ropes fall

& battles gum
into our fillings

each of us ringing
inaudibly

more noise to eradicate
but must first find

capturing the length
of evening with

our kites
up in the smoke

circling us but for

cordial disappearances

& a garish
fucked-out light

*

fables rot
in a slow storm

how night dabs its
cold paws out & rips

a hole in the street

shaking fits again

oblivious
to the umbrella
of weather

with cigarettes in bed
under a big grizzly rug

what we are
forbidden from

startles the fence
closer

lingering ferry slag
gulls hang onto

more bears out
from the woods

but what can they
want with us

a hamlet of
unschooled truants

singing choruses
sitting their own exams

diacritical marks
cleaved off from
any history

scored with
a rector's noxious whistling

the pastoral smarts

cold urn teetering
still unravished

*

using a trapdoor to show
how these levers work

or work against us
soft snare beats

click at the window

grinding us out
as through a sieve

*

our hammering finds us
an ocean of this at our shins

a throng of birds
drags down the chopper

forest lit with crooked
deforested light

up off
the shiny mud

gravestones without number

numbers without name

*

so angels of consumption
& gout

of a future anterior

this sweeping blue fire

making us up against

fortress walls forgoing

a dwindling legion of thread
between swamps crossed

to pikes
as if on an isthmus

your noise is here

but where are you

      *

no era
just the incantation
of long meadow-like strings

coughing their tracers
between each step

white spool of our kite freed
but what returned

was the roof floating down
from upriver

& three days of hake in the sink

*

copped methods as
an old math pours on & on

strychnine in those seduced
& planks for the just dead

footpaths marked by
false stars

it gathers up in
this bladder of light

there on the corner you are
your shirt open a bit in your blue skirt
& flat owl shoes

any train carrying
the dreaded awake
over ratty tracks

now curry favor
block the scene

& so
suffer yourself

A Droplight

it's coffee grounds in the coffee
somebody un-

filling
of sleep & nerves

I like your pajamas
& the way you go

into the water
with them on & on out

ship steam is cold

the berries in the pie
on the sill are hot

& I can't keep
apologizing

without knowing
what exactly for

hugged
under my ribs ticking
as a cursed hoof

ocean redeeming
its birds nightlong

the sluggish cross-hatched dusk
sea-roiling prow-coppering dusk

ice-foiling & under-grassy dusk

pissing off the bow into
the salty lake foam

from a wooden palate
with mice in the engine
& maggots at the cornmeal

wanting the shoals to phosphoresce
so bad my spine twists to rope

*

memory does its little valve work:
pickup truck from the thornbreak

hidden ivy
corpulent reeds

a message dropped
at the saint's beer

saying we're not sorry
it had to be exacted this way

*

from aluminum sky
into mere photographs

where one's just dragged off
out of their house

& then this tiny town
gets its quiet going again

first dust scritch
before a diamond needle
tricks into the groove

goodbye pigeons
in the loop

what you can't hear
is what's watching you

                    *

it's a bad history
full of a long lesson

so you bring it aboard
no matter your former

destinations
or colony fables

trade us out
under the freezing viaducts

ambulances drifting around
like gurneys

dogs in the street & one ghost
just standing there

like a stork won't flick down
her cigarette

        *

twilight
your coiled up moon

came in with the mail

condensation
on the white windows

thunder in clipping cold strings

I am sorry I want
a sloe plum

& an armada
to march invisibly without

clematis or sprawl

or stone bucket

a little bucket for
foxed milk

here it says
come here

*

a radial droplight
lowered from clouds

its silvery skin
gets its light on us

so we said to the wind
said no derision

spilled a squished currant
into what misremembers us

as superfluous chatter
with coins heavy over the eyes

knowing I keep
asking the dead
the wrong set of questions

*

bees in the hold
a lake of bees

at graveyard fence rows
more bees & it's a storm

a slow wall of bees
listening to us

write us down
under gimmicky lights

A Saint among the
Stragglers' Beds

another code fathoms forth
& its messenger at the river

cored like an apple

I guide them to a wind
which summons the forest

from a man named Ashley
& a boy he called Small

by lampmatch
to hydrangeas

a fold for disappeared ones

as this ink marks
a six on the back of your hand

it smudges your chin in the rain
& what they've said breaks into bats

what collects in hollows
un-gums out into the wake

so it goes

record sleeves
flooded factions
oceanic cutters

& news factories
giving constables
back to the loam

just when she tied her hair up
with a pencil

who she was with
fell through the floor

as the candle sputtered
& went out with

what armors
the birds

            *

now the hushed get
even quieter

& its attendant coughs so hard
the elevator vanishes

botched trade winds drop
an insignia to know

which spot's ours

the wind's not gone
it's just gone inside for a while

as inspectors chalk out
what they claim to forge
into your familiars

the saint's pocket watch
with a baby snake for hands

his music switches up
with a whipping

aspirin uncoils in soda water
as a child rows out
into the marsh fast as egrets

*

they'd disbursed powdery lime
into cracks in the earth

& ants form their own weapon

what we request
won't let us the way in

a crumbling blockade
to cast off the lantern

& chart your way into
bulrush & sedge

our messenger with
a dime to mark her egress

owned up with matches
now clobbering horizon stars

   *

water as it cuts through black tea
the train steadies green weather against it

darkness not as deep
as it looks in the photographs

shore breakers fog up
the reedy fens

how to calm the blood
without undressing

before the saint
among the stragglers' beds

*

mute lords
with brandy
thus toppled

using the steam
as a fixative

& the winding sheet
as a flag

using the butcher
for an alibi

to disappear you must
tunnel discreet

descrying over nightfall
with unclogged wind

this coast is longer than a train track
needing coarse woolen cloth &

the clothes you're in
so needing a bad song
to whistle what's known

but may stick
to another's mouth

*

listening to our wrist blood
as if it were birds in there

we follow each other's eyes
without turning around

had known
sentinels by the color
of their horrible hands

& knew mail carriers
from their teeth clicks

so mistook the curtains
for a way through

                    *

we'd fastened keys to our heels

quick oars
a slow lighthouse light

twine better than dogs
dogs better than accomplices

rickety carousel & cement truck shadows
from lost books of phantom noise

cloudscent to water
coins for coffee or pie

a corridor in its smock of
don't come all the way in

                    *

little star of salt
inside the mouth

if images are what
history decays into

we bring our enemies
home

Upholsterers' Moon

a brief history
of rain

collects what the eye
brings down

what animals sleep under

buzz-snap buzzing
in the vacancy sign

at the horseshoe-shaped
meadow's bog

a bed as a rampart

no more unburied travelers
cutting down night

with their shoes
& socks & stockings & noise

stockyard & upholsterers' moon

a button
to button up

lightning stuck in the pond
to throw a bit of dark all over us

& you know where to find me

here in the signature made small
spilled into shadow

   *

so then the moon
drifting way too close
gets leaky

going through treeline when
a voice in the radio
accidentally says your name

*

lying might ferry us through
several parts of the month

a little blood on the underside
of a toilet seat

this kitchen window is
saying something

so we should learn to listen
with the palms of our hands

fish pulled into the drinking water
sucked into our sinks

a glass of lake

& I talk too long on the message machine
I forget what I really wanted to say

that Max Roach is dead
goodbye Max Roach go softly
into the ground or grassy airs

*

now a dog is stranded on a raft
in flood muck true

its littermates long dead
true

swallows gather up in the air again like
a bushel to pull the cartoon curtains shut

nothing against us
standing out here

waiting with Declan & cigarettes
for any bus

crooked city
we're sleeping more here

less where the librarian is so lovely I trip
& start coughing

old sea goes frothing forth
an opening in the floor of the room

no school in the floods
flood's in the school

you know this game do you

     *

now the moon gets out of the blankets

& starts its shopping cart wobble
mistaking us for fields

we're just dogs at the downy feathers
& icy stuttering soon-to-be offal

trainyard sleeping cars sleeping
bickering in the bags & bagged

*

left the machines out & on
& hidden beneath mailboxes

truants do their listening
through the pads of their feet

water in them is its own
set of messages like

radio waves but chalkier
already inside us now

   *

fat dinosaur plants
surround the wolves on a raft of lilacs

unfreezing mud gathers
on slender meadow boards

horseflies do their weaving
& trees list

above thieves in the clearing
enlisting radios

as phones
as nets

so it works us
lung-like

*

now voices gob up the line

his red jacket pulled
from swamps

saying flowers bunch together
tiny leaves get the tremolo

I wake in rushes
& hollow out the bog

with my phone
as compartments in the moon
flicker on

    *

a thimble note tied to a leaf
falls before us
reads

triptych missing
in our year of the lord's

sleep-deprived amblers
these skinny beds
of the wandered away

& the knife we thought carried the virus
carried the virus

   *

hiding in the dumbwaiter
for ten minutes or a week

raccoons sniff out a hiss
as bivouac winds

give us their names

they hobble a coffin over the pigeony
cardboarded-over muck

a shoe pulled clean away I like
how you hop hop & the pall-
bearers are doing what's to be done

but carefully so

Cold Faction

three men already four
pitchers deep

one with a shovel rests it
on the casket & won't re-
commence the digging

till the dead start to
put their clothing back on

take their sketches
to a pawn

it's here the yellow eyes
of the so-called

dead turn on like
bus engines

& we have a little
bourbon

we have a
little more bourbon

now water & back
& a tarantella comes
apart around us

& somebody gets up to dance
with another body you don't know

slowing down now
another

the trees palsy
to our bad lines

a flood to
a cold faction

four dead cats
under blackbirds in a row

that cawing brings up the blood
how storms bring down the street

sparrow feather in your lung
you could see it in the x-ray

after they dragged a body in

none of us know this song backwards

to rebuild the slashed meadow
underground

*

so for the dead to carry us around
they're stapled to lost passwords

tricking no shame
in what we unearth

loss is a feature of what you've failed
to divide yourself from

more gossip by thumbtack
away from this now

says something other than
the dead are forever under us

& it gets its draggy nets out

*

I get a moment in the bathroom
& don't know what alone to do with it

weather's been casting spells
over this fucked up town now bored

that we can't fathom each other
let alone cesspools

reedy sloughs

spools to clouds
from all god's children
above their slant-wise
pillowy light

the maps get watery
& start moving us around like deer

                    *

what's known
fits into a single post office
in the heart of a small city

so we copy out a long apology on
paper towels from a latrine

as the sky marks a truce
with its soft insides

it's won but won't gloat
for clammy sorrow

the mailman finally
just brings me a strawberry pie
& I let the phone ring & ring it is

glorious this ringing when
the pie comes

now that bear rug's hung
from an era we no longer know
to serve by genuflection or speech

I go by Edgar Huntly now

fritz cove road
dwindles down
to a patch of currants

we keep the yellow off our necks
& line up for the hills to rename us

I go by Edgar Huntly now

I go all over with this
singing it now

                    *

woods do that tugging
& put a watch on your brothers

so how do you keep a river
out of your house

as the thieves just walk into the ditch
& lie down when the rains become a broom

*

until cemetery groundskeepers
met him in the back of the bar

he asked me to
hold the payphone receiver

while I was standing with my dog

what song drifts into you

what bad song drifts from
you to somebody else

down storm drains
the pull of our sacked city
gushing in pieces

everybody saying goodbye & goodnight
& off with you then

off with you & yours
& fondly out off with you

I'll say off with you now
oh be gone with you
off & away

nightgowns & hymnals
of the so-called living

tread nightly off

some chubby white reservoir
towers are here but are
we here also

dragoons in daguerreotypes carried
out no war's thieves'

songs' words'
rhythms are this way known

                    *

on the phonebooth in the dream
no I'm on top

& the river flood strands a mutt
I don't know on a porch

but it's not river water proper
it's fish & shit & people face down
floating by

telephone lines
& some wires cabled into the muck

no horror to come it is here & so
my radio clicks on

                *

nimbus-ed the window
with a cigarette lighter
she'd climbed out of

it was one of those motel rooms
with adjoining doors

I give it a little knock
it gives me
a little knock back

*

this girl maybe seven
maybe eight

in the tavern
she's all tooth & freckles asks

what's your dog's name
it's Bella

& wants to know
if my dog has a heart too

so brindle Bella lets this kid lift her
to her small ear & says

I can hear something
in your dog

                    *

her mother's in hip waders
fishing around with a huge willowy net

the little girl & her two sisters
yes the messengers
now sing

the mice scurry but are actually
rearranging to say something
it's just I cannot know what

holding my cellphone as a lantern
& dusk is gone

her mother stays out in the waters
but the music of its lap
starts sloshing going slap-slap

so thread the pedal steel & voice
lovely at breaking its own register

vipers do this
Geeshie Wiley can too

A Brief History of Gossip

laughter carries its own
corpulent history in gravel

how light is projected
from bored stars

a little story
with no yarn
no doorknob

because wind
is a deterrent

& digging
a method for

distracting the living
from the dead

gossip is the break
in a forest

where the recording devices
click back on

to show us how sadness
works in a loop

*

the light you see
cannot hear you

a blessing cameras refuse

what follows us in
is the long white cables
we've hooked cities to

the trees undoing what

we claim to have claimed

deeds gone

what we said we'd do
gone also

*

I too have come between ice shelves
to debase the coinage

or at least
songline the blooded now
known to your forebears

their fables no longer what's
used to keep us here

we are used to keep us here

river water deep in us
like declension

it's not as though
spiders follow up with us

now the sky gets blacker
because that's what it's made of

what we cite
labors under the force
of naming it

beyond pallbearers
no history makes
itself up

what we mean with history
just a treadle
for hagiography's dumbshow

*

rivering through your lines
to a digger of grief under the ice

that black box is now frozen
gerrymandering the lord's
lords' experience with the bad story
we'd whisper along the scanned notes

maybe decoration day meant bitters
& a coleopterous scattering
or how to cozen your four fingers
forward into the purse dangling down

a satchel of diamonds
I'm right about that

that's the transom
an itty bit ajar